THE CIRCLE GAME

BOOKS BY MARGARET ATWOOD

FICTION

The Edible Woman (1969)
Surfacing (1972)
Lady Oracle (1976)
Dancing Girls (1977)
Life Before Man (1979)
Bodily Harm (1981)
Murder in the Dark (1983)
Bluebeard's Egg (1983)
The Handmaid's Tale (1985)
Cat's Eye (1988)
Wilderness Tips (1991)
Good Bones (1992)
The Robber Bride (1993)
Good Bones and Simple
  Murders (1994)
Alias Grace (1996)
The Blind Assassin (2000)
Oryx and Crake (2003)
The Penelopiad (2005)
The Tent (2006)
Moral Disorder (2006)
The Year of the Flood (2009)

FOR CHILDREN

Up in the Tree (1978)
Anna's Pet [with Joyce
  Barkhouse] (1980)
For the Birds (1990)
Princess Prunella and the Purple
  Peanut (1995)
Rude Ramsay and the Roaring
  Radishes (2003)
Bashful Bob and Doleful
  Dorinda (2004)
Wandering Wenda and Widow
  Wallop's Wunderground
  Washery (2011)

NONFICTION

Survival: A Thematic Guide to
  Canadian Literature (1972)
Days of the Rebels 1815–1840 (1977)
Second Words (1982)
Strange Things: The Malevolent North
  in Canadian Literature (1996)
Two Solicitudes: Conversations [with
  Victor-Lévy Beaulieu] (1998)
Negotiating with the Dead: A Writer
  on Writing (2002)
Moving Targets: Writing with Intent
  1982–2004 (2004)
Curious Pursuits: Occasional
  Writing (2005)
Writing with Intent: Essays, Reviews,
  Personal Prose 1983–2005 (2005)
Payback: Debt and the Shadow Side of
  Wealth (2008)
In Other Worlds: SF and the Human
  Imagination (2011)

POETRY

Double Persephone (1961)
The Circle Game (1966)
The Animals in That Country (1968)
The Journals of Susanna Moodie (1970)
Procedures for Underground (1970)
Power Politics (1971)
You Are Happy (1974)
Selected Poems (1976)
Two-Headed Poems (1978)
True Stories (1981)
Interlunar (1984)
Selected Poems II: Poems Selected and
  New 1976–1986 (1986)
Morning in the Burned House (1995)
Eating Fire: Selected Poems
  1965–1995 (1998)
The Door (2007)

THE CIRCLE GAME
MARGARET ATWOOD

LIST

The sequence *The Circle Game* first appeared as a series of lithographs by Charles
Pachter. Some of the other poems first appeared in *Alaska Review*, *The Canadian
Forum*, *Edge*, *English*, *Evidence*, *Kayak*, *Prism International*, and *Queen's Quarterly*.

First published in 1966 by Contact Press
First House of Anansi Press edition in 1967

This edition published in 2012 by House of Anansi Press Inc.
houseofanansi.com

House of Anansi Press is committed to protecting our natural environment. This
book is made of material from well-managed FSC®-certified forests, recycled
materials, and other controlled sources.

House of Anansi Press is a Global Certified Accessible™ (GCA by Benetech) publisher.
The ebook version of this book meets stringent accessibility standards and is available
to readers with print disabilities.

27 26 24 24 23   4 5 6 7 8

Library and Archives Canada Cataloguing in Publication Data

Atwood, Margaret, 1939–
The circle game / Margaret Atwood ; introduction by
Suzanne Buffam.

Poems.
Issued also in electronic format.
ISBN 978-1-77089-278-1

I. Title.

PS8501.T86C5 2012   C811'.54   C2012-903621-8

Library of Congress Control Number: 2012939949

Cover design: Brian Morgan
Cover illustration: Genevieve Simms
Typesetting: Marijke Friesen

*House of Anansi Press is grateful for the privilege to work on and create from the
Traditional Territory of many Nations, including the Anishinabeg, the Wendat, and the
Haudenosaunee, as well as the Treaty Lands of the Mississaugas of the Credit.*

 Canada Council   Conseil des Arts   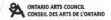 ONTARIO ARTS COUNCIL
for the Arts   du Canada   CONSEIL DES ARTS DE L'ONTARIO

*We acknowledge for their financial support of our publishing program the Canada
Council for the Arts, the Ontario Arts Council, and the Government of Canada.*

Printed and bound in Canada

MIX
Paper from
responsible sources
FSC   FSC® C103567
www.fsc.org

INTRODUCTION
BY SUZANNE BUFFAM

I met Margaret Atwood once, nearly two decades ago, at a literary awards ceremony in a courthouse made of glass. She was filling in for the MC, I believe, or perhaps an honoree, who had suddenly fallen ill. I was a borderline Creative Writing major with a minor in Women's Studies, staffing a table for the local feminist bookstore, and I made it my evening's mission to shake her hand. At some point during our pleasant exchange outside the ladies' room, she made one particularly droll remark, the substance of which, alas, has long since escaped me. What I do remember, however, is her tone: intimate, knowing, in the manner of a witty aside, as if she had invited me, however briefly, into the private parentheses of her thoughts.

According to *The Handbook of Effective Writing*, composed by the felicitously-named Walter Kay Smart, the thoughts presented in a parenthetical interruption "are not crucial to the sentence, but directly or moderately relate to the primary statement." Where dashes direct our attention to what they set off — look at me! they seem to insist — the more diffident parentheses enclose what one may safely choose to ignore. In poetry, however, where even the most innocuous piece of punctuation aspires to dramatic effect, anyone who overlooks a mere parenthetical might very well miss the whole point.

Atwood, as readers of this book will quickly see for themselves, is a philosopher of the parenthetical. Take a look at the opening poem. "This Is a Photograph of Me," the speaker claims in the title, and what follows, for the first half of the poem anyway, is a sort of Self Portrait As Landscape, missing any discernible human figure. From the depths of a blurry print, we make out part of a tree, a small frame house, and in the background, a lake, some low hills. Halfway through this muted pastoral, however, the speaker steps into the icy waters of an unsettling parenthetical from which she never steps out:

> (The photograph was taken
> the day after I drowned.
>
> I am in the lake, in the centre
> of the picture, just under the surface . . .

Every time I re-read this passage, I'm struck by the sudden directness of this disclosure, an effect generated, it seems to me, as much by the opening of that parenthesis as by the unexpected arrival of the first person into the poem. But the parentheses do not close here. Having pulled us at last into the circle of her confidence, Atwood's dead girl has more to say, even if what she says concerns the very difficulty of saying anything at all, precisely, about her condition:

> It is difficult to say where
> precisely, or to say
> how large or small I am . . .

Never mind that she has just told us where to look for her, "in the lake, in the centre / of the picture." Atwood's posthumous speaker understands the unreliability of perspective, and with it, the subjective nature of centrality itself. No hysterical spectre of feminine victimhood, this dispassionate ghost sounds less like the tragic heroine of a gothic romance than a pontificating existential phenomenologist. As Atwood continues to unfold her origami-like aside, the speaker's perspective shifts yet again, first to a brief lesson on optics and refraction, and finally to a sort of promise and challenge to readers seeking to locate the author under the surface of the text:

the effect of water
on light is a distortion

but if you look long enough,
eventually
you will be able to see me.)

I envy writers who are capable of such subtle and mercurial tonal shifts. Claiming the omniscient authority of the dead, Atwood establishes, in this opening, scene-stealing parenthetical, a remarkable authority of voice that she maintains, with hardly a misstep, throughout the entire collection. In poem after poem, we see the young Atwood testing the edges of articulable thought. Not only are her parentheticals utterly "crucial to the sentence(s)" they interrupt, but, like secrets whispered between a pair of cupped hands, they embed an urgent intimacy within the overall tact and perspicacity of her poetic project. The fact that she was a mere twenty-seven years old when she first published these poems only makes one marvel further at this achievement.

Nothing is quite what it seems in the haunted world of these poems. Every landscape conceals a dark history. Optical illusions, viewed from a new angle, resemble prophetic projections. Canny observations give rise to uncanny asides. The world of appearances and apparitions contained within this book harbours portents of supernatural menace, but also, occasionally, glimmers of transcendence and hope. If you think you understand what you see on the surface, caution Atwood's fathomless parentheticals, keep looking.

For J.

CONTENTS

THE CIRCLE GAME

THIS IS A PHOTOGRAPH OF ME

It was taken some time ago.
At first it seems to be
a smeared
print: blurred lines and grey flecks
blended with the paper;

then, as you scan
it, you see in the left-hand corner
a thing that is like a branch: part of a tree
(balsam or spruce) emerging
and, to the right, halfway up
what ought to be a gentle
slope, a small frame house.

In the background there is a lake,
and beyond that, some low hills.

(The photograph was taken
the day after I drowned.

I am in the lake, in the centre
of the picture, just under the surface.

It is difficult to say where
precisely, or to say
how large or small I am:
the effect of water
on light is a distortion

but if you look long enough,
eventually
you will be able to see me.)

AFTER THE FLOOD, WE

We must be the only ones
left, in the mist that has risen
everywhere as well
as in these woods

I walk across the bridge
towards the safety of high ground
(the tops of the trees are like islands)

gathering the sunken
bones of the drowned mothers
(hard and round in my hands)
while the white mist washes
around my legs like water;

fish must be swimming
down in the forest beneath us,
like birds, from tree to tree
and a mile away
the city, wide and silent,
is lying lost, far undersea.

You saunter beside me, talking
of the beauty of the morning,
not even knowing
that there has been a flood,

tossing small pebbles
at random over your shoulder
into the deep thick air,

not hearing the first stumbling
footsteps of the almost-born
coming (slowly) behind us,
not seeing
the almost-human
brutal faces forming
(slowly)
out of stone.

A MESSENGER

The man came from nowhere
and is going nowhere

one day he suddenly appeared
outside my window
suspended in the air
between the ground and the tree bough

I once thought all encounters
were planned:
newspaper boys passing
in the street, with cryptic
headlines, waitresses and their coded
menus, women standing in streetcars
with secret packages, were sent to
me. And gave some time
to their deciphering

but this one is clearly
accidental; clearly this one is

no green angel, simple black and white
fiend; no ordained
messenger; merely
a random face
revolving outside the window

and if no evident abstract
significance, then
something as contingent
as a candidate for marriage
in this district of exacting neighbours:
not meant for me personally
but generic: to be considered
from all angles (origin; occupation;
aim in life); identification
papers examined; if appropriate,
conversed with; when
he can be made to descend.

Meanwhile, I wonder

which of the green or
black and white
myths he swallowed by mistake
is feeding on him like a tapeworm
has raised him from the ground
and brought him to this window

swivelling from some invisible rope
his particular features
fading day by day
                    his eyes melted
                    first; Thursday
                    his flesh became translucent
shouting at me
(specific) me
desperate messages with his
obliterated mouth

in a silent language

EVENING TRAINSTATION, BEFORE DEPARTURE

It seems I am always
moving

(and behind me the lady
slumped in darkness
on a wooden bench
in the park, thinking
of nothing: the screams
of the children
going down the slide
behind her, topple her mind
into deep trenches)

moving

(and in front of me the man
standing in a white room
three flights up, a razor
(or is the evening
a razor) poised in his hand
considering
what it is for)

move with me.

Here I am in
a pause in space
hunched on the edge
of a tense suitcase
(in which there is a gathering
of soiled clothing, plastic bottles,
scissors, barbed wire
and a lady
and a man)

In a minute everything will begin
to move: the man
will tumble from the room, the lady
will take the razor in her black-gloved hand

and I will get on the train
and move elsewhere once more.

At the last station
under the electric clock
there was a poster: *Where?*
part of some obscure campaign;

at this one there is a loudspeaker
that calls the names and places
(the sounds like static; the silences
thin as razorblades between)

at the next one there will be
a lady and a man,
some other face or evidence
to add to the
collection in my suitcase.

The world is turning
me into evening.

I'm almost ready:
this time it will be far.

I move
and live on the edges
(what edges)
I live
on all the edges there are.

AN ATTEMPTED SOLUTION FOR CHESS PROBLEMS

My younger sister at the chessboard
ponders her next move
the arrangement of her empire
(crosslegged on the floor)

while below her in the cellar
the embroidered costumes, taken
from her mother's storage trunks
and lined against the walls
lose their stiff directions in
the instant that she hesitates
above the armies

The shadows of the chessmen
stretch, fall across her: she
is obsessed by history;
each wooden totem rises
like the cairn of an event

(but)

Outside the windows of this room
the land unrolls without landmark
a meshing of green on green, the inner
membrane of the gaping moment
opening around a sun that is
a hole burnt in the sky.

The house recoils
from the brightedged vacancy
of leaves, into itself: the cellar
darkness looming with archaic
silver clocks, brocaded chairs, the fading echoes
of a hunting horn.

The white king moves
by memories and procedures
and corners
no final ending but
a stalemate,
forcing her universe to his
geographies: the choice imposes
vestiges of black and white
ruled squares on the green landscape,

and her failed solution
has planted the straight rows
of an armoured wood patrolled by wooden
kings and queens
hunting the mechanical unicorn
under a coin-round sun.

Her step on the stairs
sounds through the concrete mazes.

In her cellar the mailed
costumes rustle
waiting to be put on.

IN MY RAVINES

This year in my ravines
it was warm for a long time
although the leaves fell early
and my old men, re-
membering themselves
walked waist-high through the
yellow grass
in my ravines, through
alders and purple
fireweed, with burrs
catching on their sleeves,

watching the small boys climbing
in the leafless trees
or throwing pebbles
at tin cans floating
in the valley creek, or following
the hard paths worn by former
walkers or the hooves
of riding-stable horses

and at night
they slept under the bridges
of the city in my (still)
ravines

old men, ravelled as thistles
their clothing gone to seed
their beards cut stubble

while the young boys
climbed and swung
above them wildly
in the leafless eyelid
veins and branches
of a bloodred night
falling, bursting purple
as ancient rage, in

old men's
dreams of slaughter
dreams of
(impossible)
flight.

A DESCENT THROUGH THE CARPET

i

Outside the window the harbour is
a surface only with mountains and
sailboats and
destroyers
        depthless on the glass

but inside there's a
patterned carpet on the floor
        maroon green purple
        brittle fronds and hard
        petals

It makes the sea
accessible
as I stretch out with these
convoluted gardens
at eyelevel,
        the sun
filtering down through the windows
of this housetop aquarium

and in the green halflight
I drift down past the
marginal orchards branched
colourful
        feathered
                and overfilled
        with giving

into the long iceage
                     the pressures
of winter
             the snowfall endless in the sea

ii

But not
rocked not cradled not forgetful:
there are no
sunken kingdoms no
edens in the waste ocean

among the shattered
memories of battles

only the cold jewelled symmetries
of the voracious eater
the voracious eaten

the dream creatures that glow
sulphurous in darkness or
flash like neurons
are blind, insatiable, all
gaping jaws and famine

and here
to be aware is
to know total
               fear.

iii

Gunshot
      outside the window
            nine o'clock
Somehow I sit up
breaking the membrane of water

Emerged and
beached on the carpet
breathing this air once more
I stare

at the sackful of scales and

my fisted
hand
     my skin
holds

      remnants of ancestors

      fossil bones and fangs

acknowledgement:

I was born
     dredged up from time
and harboured
the night these wars began.

PLAYING CARDS

In this room we are always in:

tired with all the other games
we get out cards and play
at double
solitaire:
the only thing
either of us might win.

There's a queen.
Or rather two of them
joined at the waist, or near
(you can't tell where
exactly, under the thick
brocaded costume)
or is it one
woman with two heads?
Each has hair drawn back
made of lines
and a half-smile that is part
of a set pattern.

Each holds a golden flower
with five petals, ordered
and unwilting.

Outside there is a lake
or this time is it a street

There's a king (or kings)
too, with a beard to show
he is a man
and something abstract
in his hand
that might be either
a sceptre or a sword.

The colour doesn't matter,
black or red:
there's little choice between
heart and spade.
The important things
are the flowers and the swords;
but they stay flat,
are cardboard.

Outside there is a truck
or possibly a motorboat

and in this lighted room
across the table, we
confront each other

wearing no costumes.

You have nothing
that serves the function of a sceptre
and I have
certainly
no flowers.

MAN WITH A HOOK

This man I
know (about a year
ago, when he was young) blew
his arm off in the cellar
making bombs
to explode the robins
on the lawns.

Now he has a hook
instead of hand;

It is an ingenious
gadget, and comes
with various attachments:
knife for meals,
pink plastic hand for everyday
handshakes, black stuffed leather glove
for social functions.

I attempt pity

But, Look, he says, glittering
like a fanatic, My hook
is an improvement:

        and to demonstrate
lowers his arm: the steel question-
mark turns and opens,
and from his burning
cigarette
            unscrews
and holds the delicate
ash: a thing
precise
my clumsy tender-
skinned pink fingers
couldn't do.

THE CITY PLANNERS

Cruising these residential Sunday
streets in dry August sunlight:
what offends us is
the sanities:
the houses in pedantic rows, the planted
sanitary trees, assert
levelness of surface like a rebuke
to the dent in our car door.
No shouting here, or
shatter of glass; nothing more abrupt
than the rational whine of a power mower
cutting a straight swath in the discouraged grass.

But though the driveways neatly
sidestep hysteria
by being even, the roofs all display
the same slant of avoidance to the hot sky,
certain things;
the smell of spilled oil a faint
sickness lingering in the garages,
a splash of paint on brick surprising as a bruise,
a plastic hose poised in a vicious
coil; even the too-fixed stare of the wide windows

give momentary access to
the landscape behind or under
the future cracks in the plaster

when the houses, capsized, will slide
obliquely into the clay seas, gradual as glaciers
that right now nobody notices.

That is where the City Planners
with the insane faces of political conspirators
are scattered over unsurveyed
territories, concealed from each other,
each in his own private blizzard;

guessing directions, they sketch
transitory lines rigid as wooden borders
on a wall in the white vanishing air

tracing the panic of suburb
order in a bland madness of snows.

ON THE STREETS, LOVE

On the streets
love
these days
is a matter for
either scavengers
(turning death to life) or
(turning life
to death) for predators

(The billboard lady
with her white enamel
teeth and red
enamel claws, is after

      the men
      when they pass her
      never guess they have brought her
      to life, or that her
      body's made of cardboard, or in her
      veins flows the drained
      blood of their desire)
(Look, the grey man
his footsteps soft
as flan-
nel, glides from his poster

and the voracious women, seeing
him so trim,
edges clear as cut paper
eyes clean
and sharp as lettering,
want to own him
    . . . are you dead? are you dead?
    they say, hoping . . .)

Love, what are we to do
on the streets these days
and how am I
to know that you
and how are you to know
that I, that

we are not parts of those
people, scraps glued together
waiting for a chance
to come to life

(One day
I'll touch the warm
flesh of your throat, and hear
a faint crackle of paper

or you, who think
that you can read my mind
from the inside out, will taste the
black ink on my tongue, and find
the fine print written
just beneath my skin.)

EVENTUAL PROTEUS

I held you
through all your shifts
of structure: while your bones turned
from caved rock back to marrow,
the dangerous
fur faded to hair
the bird's cry died in your throat
the treebark paled from your skin
the leaves from your eyes

till you limped back again
to daily man:
a lounger on streetcorners
in iron-shiny gabardine
a leaner on stale tables;
at night a twitching sleeper
dreaming of crumbs and rinds and a sagging woman,
caged by a sour bed.

The early
languages are obsolete.

These days we keep
our weary distances:
sparring in the vacant spaces
of peeling rooms
and rented minutes, climbing
all the expected stairs, our voices
abraded with fatigue,
our bodies wary.

Shrunk by my disbelief
you cannot raise
the green gigantic skies, resume
the legends of your disguises:

this shape is final.

Now, when you come near
attempting towards me across
these sheer cavernous
inches of air

your flesh has no more stories
or surprises;

my face flinches
under the sarcastic
tongues of your estranging
fingers,
the caustic remark of your kiss.

A MEAL

We sit at a clean table
eating thoughts from clean plates

and see, there is my heart
germfree, and transparent as glass

and there is my brain, pure
as cold water in the china
bowl of my skull

and you are talking
with words that fall spare
on the ear like the metallic clink
of knife and fork.

Safety by all means;
so we eat and drink
remotely, so we pick
the abstract bone

but something is hiding
somewhere
in the scrubbed bare
cupboard of my body
flattening itself
against a shelf
and feeding
on other people's leavings

a furtive insect, sly and primitive
the necessary cockroach
in the flesh
that nests in dust.

It will sidle out
when the lights have all gone off
in this bright room

(and you can't
crush it in the dark then
my friend or search it out
with your mind's hands that smell
of insecticide and careful soap)

In spite of our famines
it keeps itself alive

: how it gorges on a few
unintentional
spilled crumbs of love

THE CIRCLE GAME

i

The children on the lawn
joined hand to hand
go round and round

each arm going into
the next arm, around
full circle
until it comes
back into each of the single
bodies again

They are singing, but
not to each other:
their feet move
almost in time to the singing

We can see
the concentration on
their faces, their eyes
fixed on the empty
moving spaces just in
front of them.

We might mistake this
tranced moving for joy
but there is no joy in it

We can see (arm in arm)
as we watch them go
round and round
intent, almost
studious (the grass
underfoot ignored, the trees
circling the lawn
ignored, the lake ignored)
that the whole point

for them
of going round and round
is (faster
    slower)
going round and round

ii

Being with you
here, in this room

is like groping through a mirror
whose glass has melted
to the consistency
of gelatin

You refuse to be
(and I)
an exact reflection, yet
will not walk from the glass,
be separate.

Anyway, it is right
that they have put
so many mirrors here
(chipped, hung crooked)
in this room with its high transom
and empty wardrobe; even
the back of the door
has one.

There are people in the next room
arguing, opening and closing drawers
(the walls are thin)

You look past me, listening
to them, perhaps, or
watching
your own reflection somewhere
behind my head,
over my shoulder

You shift, and the bed
sags under us, losing its focus

There is someone in the next room

There is always

(your face
remote, listening)

someone in the next room.

iii

However,
in all their games
there seems
to be some reason

however
abstract they
at first appear

When we read them legends
in the evening
of monstrous battles, and secret
betrayals in the forest
and brutal deaths,

they scarcely listened;
one yawned and fidgeted; another
chewed the wooden handle
of a hammer;
the youngest one examined
a slight cut on his toe,

and we wondered how
they could remain
completely without fear
or even interest
as the final sword slid through
the dying hero.

The next night
walking along the beach

we found the trenches
they had been making:
fortified with pointed sticks
driven into the sides
of their sand moats

and a lake-enclosed island
with no bridges:

a last attempt
(however
eroded by the water
in an hour)
to make
maybe, a refuge human
and secure from the reach

of whatever walks along
(sword hearted)
these night beaches.

iv

Returning to the room:
I notice how
all your word-
plays, calculated ploys
of the body, the witticisms
of touch, are now
attempts to keep me
at a certain distance
and (at length) avoid
admitting I am here

I watch you
watching my face
indifferently
yet with the same taut curiosity
with which you might regard
a suddenly discovered part
of your own body:
a wart perhaps,

and I remember that
you said
in childhood you were
a tracer of maps
(not making but) moving
a pen or a forefinger
over the courses of the rivers,
the different colours
that mark the rise of mountains;
a memorizer
of names (to hold
these places
in their proper places)

So now you trace me
like a country's boundary
or a strange new wrinkle in
your own wellknown skin

and I am fixed, stuck
down on the outspread map
of this room, of your mind's continent
        (here and yet not here, like
        the wardrobe and the mirrors
        the voices through the wall
        your body ignored on the bed),

transfixed
by your eyes'
cold blue thumbtacks

v

The children like the block
of grey stone that was once a fort
but now is a museum:

especially
they like the guns
and the armour brought from
other times and countries

and when they go home
their drawings will be full
for some days, of swords
archaic sunburst maces
broken spears
and vivid red explosions.

While they explore
the cannons
(they aren't our children)

we walk outside along
the earthworks, noting
how they are crumbling
under the unceasing
attacks of feet and flower roots;

The weapons
that were once outside
sharpening themselves on war
are now indoors
there, in the fortress,
fragile
in glass cases;

Why is it
(I'm thinking
of the careful moulding
round the stonework archways)
that in this time, such
elaborate defences keep
things that are no longer
(much)
worth defending?

vi

And you play the safe game
the orphan game

the ragged winter game
that says, I am alone

(hungry: I know you want me
to play it also)

the game of the waif who stands
at every picture window,

shivering, pinched nose pressed
against the glass, the snow
collecting on his neck,
watching the happy families

(a game of envy)

Yet he despises them: they are so
Victorian Christmas-card:
the cheap paper shows
under the pigments of
their cheerful fire-
places and satin-
ribboned suburban laughter
and they have their own forms
of parlour
games: father and mother
playing father and mother

He's glad
to be left
out by himself
in the cold

(hugging himself).

When I tell you this,
you say (with a smile fake
as a tinsel icicle):

You do it too.

Which in some ways
is a lie, but also I suppose
is right, as usual:

although I tend to pose
in other seasons
outside other windows.

vii

Summer again;
in the mirrors of this room
the children wheel, singing
the same song;

This casual bed
scruffy as dry turf,
the counterpane
rumpled with small burrows, is
their grassy lawn

and these scuffed walls
contain their circling trees,
that low clogged sink
their lake

(a wasp comes,
drawn by the piece of sandwich
left on the nearby beach
        (how carefully you do
        such details);
one of the children flinches
but won't let go)

You make them
turn and turn, according to
the closed rules of your games,
but there is no joy in it

and as we lie
arm in arm, neither
joined nor separate
    (your observations change me
    to a spineless woman in
    a cage of bones, obsolete fort
    pulled inside out),
our lips moving
almost in time to their singing,

listening to the opening
and closing of the drawers
in the next room

(of course there is always
danger but where
would you locate it)

(the children spin
a round cage of glass
from the warm air
with their thread-thin
insect voices)

and as we lie
here, caught
in the monotony of wandering
from room to room, shifting
the place of our defences,

I want to break
these bones, your prisoning rhythms
        (winter,
            summer)
all the glass cases,

erase all maps,
crack the protecting
eggshell of your turning
singing children:

I want the circle
broken.

CAMERA

You want this instant:
nearly spring, both of us walking,
wind blowing

walking
sunlight knitting the leaves before our eyes
the wind empty as Sunday

rain drying
in the wormy sidewalk puddles
the vestiges of night on our
lightscratched eyelids, our breezy fingers

you want to have it and so
you arrange us:

in front of a church, for perspective,
you make me stop walking
and compose me on the lawn;

you insist
that the clouds stop moving
the wind stop swaying the church
on its boggy foundations
the sun hold still in the sky

for your organized instant.

Camera man
how can I love your glass eye?

Wherever you partly are
now, look again
at your souvenir,
your glossy square of paper
before it dissolves completely:

it is the last of autumn
the leaves have unravelled

the pile of muddy rubble
in the foreground, is the church

the clothes I wore
are scattered over the lawn
my coat flaps in a bare tree

there has been a hurricane

that small black speck
travelling towards the horizon
at almost the speed of light

is me

WINTER SLEEPERS

They lie side by side
under a thick quilt of silence.
The air silts up with snow.

The drifting land
merges with the inside room
gradually through the window

and the white sheet
swells and furrows
in the wind: no things
in this deep sleep are solid

only perhaps this floating
bed which holds them up, a life-
raft where they weather seas
that undulate with danger.

Under the bed the dust
eddies and collects;
dead leaves, broken
twigs, water-sodden
bones of small
animals gather
like sediment on the seafloor
under the snow.

Outside, the land
is filled with drowning men

and stretched   remote   close

beside her

he foundered and went down
some time before she knew.

SPRING IN THE IGLOO

The sun had been burning for a long time
before we saw it, and we saw it
only then because
it seared itself through the roof.

We, who thought we were living
in the centre of a vast night
and therefore spent our time
hoarding our own heat

were astonished by the light.

I made this house once
because I wanted the
coldest season, where you could be
if only by comparison, a
substitute for sun

but the earth
turns for its own reasons
ignoring mine, and these human
miscalculations

and so we are drifting
into a tepid ocean
on a shrinking piece of winter

    (for two so frozen
    this long in
    glacial innocence
    to swim would be
    implausible)

with ice the only thing
between us and disaster.

A SIBYL

Below my window
in the darkening
backyard the children
play at war
among the flowerbeds

on my shelves the bottles
accumulate
      my sibyl (every woman
      should have one) has chosen
      to live there

thin green wine bottles
emptied of small dinners
ovaltine jars, orange-brown
emptied of easy sleep

      my sibyl crouches
      in one of them
      wrinkled as a pickled
      baby, twoheaded prodigy
      at a freakfair
      hairless, her sightless
      eyes like eggwhites

I stand looking
over the fading city

she calls to me with the many
voices of the children
not I want to die
but You must die
later or sooner alas
you were born weren't you
the minutes thunder like guns
coupling won't help you
or plurality
I see it
I prophesy

but she doesn't reach me.
Old spider
sibyl, I'll
uncork you
let in a little air
or I'll ignore you.

Right now
my skin is a sack of
clever tricks, five
senses ribboned like birth-
day presents unravel
in a torn web around me

and a man dances
in my kitchen, moving
like a metronome
with hopes of staying
for breakfast in the half-empty
bottle in his pocket

There are omens of
rockets among the tricycles
I know it

time runs out
in the ticking hips of the
man whose twitching skull
jerks on loose
vertebrae in my kitchen
flower
beds predict it

the city burns with an
afterglow of explosions as the
streetlights all come on

The thing that calls itself
I
right now
doesn't care

I don't care

I leave that to my
necessary sibyl
(that's what she's for)
with her safely bottled
anguish and her glass
despair

MIGRATION: C.P.R.

i

Escaping from allegories
in the misty east, where inherited events
barnacle on the mind; where every gloved handshake
might be a finger pointing; you can't look
in store windows without seeing
reflections/ remnants of privateer
bones or methodist grandfathers with jaws
carved as wood pulpits warning
of the old evil; where not-quite-
forgotten histories
make the boards of lineal frame
farmhouses rotten

the fishermen
sit all day on old wharves facing
neither sea-
wards nor inland, mending
and untangling their old nets
of thought

and language is the law

we ran west

wanting
a place of absolute
unformed beginning

(the train
an ark
upheld on the brain's darkness)

but the inner lakes reminded
us too much of ancient oceans
first flood: blood-
enemy and substance
(was our train like
an ark or like a seasnake?

and the prairies were so nearly
empty as prehistory
that each of the
few solid objects took some great
implication, hidden but
more sudden than a signpost

(like an inscribed shard, broken bowl
dug at a desert level
where they thought
no man had been,
or a burned bone)

(every dwarf tree portentous
with twisted wisdom, though
we knew no
apples grew there

and that shape, gazing
at nothing
by a hooftrampled streamside:
it could
have been a centaur)

and even the mountains
at the approach, were
conical, iconic
again:
(tents
in the desert? triangular
ships? towers? breasts?
words)
again
these barriers

ii

Once in the pass, the steep
faulted gorges were at last
real: we
tossed our eastern
suitcases from the caboose
and all our baggage:
overboard
left in our wake
along the tracks
and (we saw) our train became
only a train, in real
danger of falling; strained
speechless through those new mountains
we stepped
unbound
into

what a free emerging
on the raw
streets and hills
without meaning
always creeping up behind us
(that cold touch on the shoulder)

our faces scraped as blank
as we could wish them

(but needing new
houses, new
dishes, new
husks)

iii

There are more secondhand
stores here than we expected:
though we brought nothing with us
(we thought)
we have begun to unpack.

A residual brass bedstead
scratched with the initials
of generic brides and grooms;
chipped squat teapots: old totemic
mothers; a boxful
of used hats.

In the forest, even
apart from the trodden
paths, we can tell (from the sawn
firstumps) that many
have passed the same way
some time before
this (hieroglyphics
carved in the bark)

Things here grow from the ground
too insistently
green to seem
spontaneous. (My skeletons, I think,
will be still
in the windows when I look,
as well as the books
and the index-
fingered gloves.)

There is also a sea
that refuses to stay in the harbour:
becomes opaque
air or throws
brown seaweeds like small drowned hands
up on these shores

(the fishermen
are casting their nets here
as well)

and blunted mountains
rolling
        (the first whales maybe?)
in the
inescapable mists.

JOURNEY TO THE INTERIOR

There are similarities
I notice: that the hills
which the eyes make flat as a wall, welded
together, open as I move
to let me through; become
endless as prairies; that the trees
grow spindly, have their roots
often in swamps; that this is a poor country;
that a cliff is not known
as rough except by hand, and is
therefore inaccessible. Mostly
that travel is not the easy going
from point to point, a dotted
line on a map, location
plotted on a square surface
but that I move surrounded by a tangle
of branches, a net of air and alternate
light and dark, at all times;
that there are no destinations
apart from this.

There are differences
of course: the lack of reliable charts;
more important, the distraction of small details:
your shoe among the brambles under the chair
where it shouldn't be; lucent
white mushrooms and a paring knife
on the kitchen table; a sentence
crossing my path, sodden as a fallen log
I'm sure I passed yesterday

                              (have I been
walking in circles again?)

but mostly the danger:
many have been here, but only
some have returned safely.

A compass is useless; also
trying to take directions
from the movements of the sun,
which are erratic;
and words here are as pointless
as calling in a vacant
wilderness.
                    Whatever I do I must
keep my head. I know
it is easier for me to lose my way
forever here, than in other landscapes

SOME OBJECTS OF WOOD AND STONE

i) Totems

We went to the park
where they kept the wooden people:
static, multiple
uprooted and trans-
planted.

Their faces were restored,
freshly-painted.
In front of them
the other wooden people
posed for each others' cameras
and nearby a new booth
sold replicas and souvenirs.

One of the people was real.
It lay on its back, smashed
by a toppling fall or just
the enduring of minor winters.
Only one of the heads had
survived intact, and it was
also beginning to decay
but there was a
life in the progressing
of old wood back to
the earth, obliteration

that the clear-hewn
standing figures lacked.

As for us, perennial watchers,
tourists of another kind
there is nothing for us to worship;

no pictures of ourselves, no blue-
sky summer fetishes, no postcards
we can either buy, or
smiling
be.

There are few totems that remain
living for us.
Though in passing,
through glass we notice

dead trees in the seared meadows
dead roots bleaching in the swamps.

ii) Pebbles

Talking was difficult. Instead
we gathered coloured pebbles
from the places on the beach
where they occurred.

They were sea-smoothed, sea-completed.
They enclosed what they intended
to mean in shapes
as random and necessary
as the shapes of words

and when finally
we spoke
the sounds of our voices fell
into the air   single and
solid and rounded and really
there
and then dulled, and then like sounds
gone,   a fistful of gathered
pebbles there was no point
in taking home, dropped on a beachful
of other coloured pebbles

and when we turned to go
a flock of small
birds flew scattered by the
fright of our sudden moving
and disappeared: hard

sea pebbles
thrown solid for an instant
against the sky

flight of words

iii) Carved Animals

The small carved
animal is passed from
hand to hand
around the circle
until the stone grows warm

touching, the hands do not know
the form of animal
which was made or
the true form of stone
uncovered

and the hands, the fingers the
hidden small bones
of the hands bend to hold the shape,
shape themselves, grow
cold with the stone's cold, grow
also animal, exchange
until the skin wonders
if stone is human

In the darkness later
and even when the animal
has gone, they keep
the image of that
inner shape

hands holding warm
hands holding
the half-formed air

PRE-AMPHIBIAN

Again so I subside
nudged by the softening
driftwood of your body
tangle on you like a water-
weed caught
on a submerged treelimb

with sleep like a swamp
growing, closing around me
sending its tendrils through the brown
sediments of darkness
where we   transmuted   are
part of this warm rotting
of vegetable flesh
this quiet spawning of roots

released
from the lucidities of day
when you are something I can
trace a line around, with eyes
cut shapes
from air, the element
where we
must calculate according to
solidities

but here I blur
into you   our breathing sinking
to green millenniums
and   sluggish   in our blood
all ancestors
are warm fish moving

The earth
shifts, bringing
the moment before focus, when
these tides recede; and we
see each other through the
hardening scales of waking

stranded, astounded
in a drying world

we flounder, the air
ungainly in our new lungs
with sunlight steaming merciless on the shores of morning

AGAINST STILL LIFE

Orange in the middle of a table:

It isn't enough
to walk around it
at a distance, saying
it's an orange:
nothing to do
with us, nothing
else: leave it alone

I want to pick it up
in my hand
I want to peel the
skin off; I want
more to be said to me
than just Orange:
want to be told
everything it has to say

And you, sitting across
the table, at a distance, with
your smile contained, and like the orange
in the sun: silent:

Your silence
isn't enough for me
now, no matter with what
contentment you fold
your hands together; I want
anything you can say
in the sunlight:

stories of your various
childhoods, aimless journeyings,
your loves; your articulate
skeleton; your posturings; your lies.

These orange silences
(sunlight and hidden smile)
make me want to
wrench you into saying;
now I'd crack your skull
like a walnut, split it like a pumpkin
to make you talk, or get
a look inside

But quietly:
if I take the orange
with care enough and hold it
gently

I may find
an egg
a sun
an orange moon
perhaps a skull; centre
of all energy
resting in my hand

can change it to
whatever I desire
it to be

and you, man, orange afternoon
lover, wherever
you sit across from me
(tables, trains, buses)

if I watch
quietly enough
and long enough

at last, you will say
(maybe without speaking)

(there are mountains
inside your skull
garden and chaos, ocean
and hurricane; certain
corners of rooms, portraits
of great-grandmothers, curtains
of a particular shade;
your deserts; your private
dinosaurs; the first
woman)

all I need to know:
tell me
everything
just as it was
from the beginning.

THE ISLANDS

There are two of them:

One larger, with steep granite
cliffs facing us, dropping sheer
to the deep lake;

the other smaller, closer
to land, with a reef running
out from it and dead trees
grey, waist-high in the water.

We know they are alone
and always will be.

The lake takes care of that
and if it went,
they would be hills
and still demand
separateness
from the eye.

Yet, standing on the cliff
(the two
of us)
on our bigger island,
looking,

we find it pleasing
(it soothes our instinct for
symmetry, proportion,
for company perhaps)

that there are two of them.

LETTERS, TOWARDS AND AWAY

i

It is not available to us
it
is not available, I said
closing my hours against you.

I live in a universe
mostly paper.
I make tents
from cancelled stamps.

Letters
are permitted but
don't touch me, I'd
crumple

I said

everything depends on you

staying away.

ii

I didn't want you to be
visible.

How could you invade
me when
I ordered you not
to

Leave my evasions
alone
stay in the borders
I've drawn, I wrote, but

you twisted your own wide spaces

and made them include me.

iii

You came easily into my house
and without being asked
washed the dirty dishes,

because you don't find
my forms of chaos,
inverted midnights
and crusted plates,
congenial:

restoring some kind of
daily normal order.

Not normal for me:

I live in a house where
beautiful clean dishes
aren't important

enough.

iv

Love is an awkward word

Not what I mean and
too much like magazine stories
in stilted dentists'
waiting rooms.
How can anyone use it?

I'd rather say
I like your
lean spine
or your eyebrows
or your shoes

but just by standing there and
being awkward

you force me to speak

love.

v

You collapse my house of cards
merely by breathing

making other places
with your hands on wood, your
feet on sand

creating with such
generosity, mountains, distances
empty beach and rocks and sunlight
as you walk
so calmly into the sea

and returning, you
taste of salt,

and put together my own
body, another

place

for me to live
in.

vi

I don't wear gratitude
well. Or hats.

What would I do with
veils and silly feathers
or a cloth rose
growing from the top of my head?

What should I do with this
peculiar furred emotion?

vii

What you invented
what you
destroyed
with your transient hands

you did so gently
I didn't notice at the time

but where is all that wall-
paper?

Now
I'm roofless:

the sky
you built for me is too
open.

Quickly,
send me some more letters.

A PLACE: FRAGMENTS

i

Here on the rim, cringing
under the cracked whip of winter
we live
in houses of ice,
but not because we want to:
in order to survive
we make what we can and have to
with what we have.

ii

Old woman I visited once
out of my way
in a little-visited province:

she had a neat
house, a clean parlour
though obsolete and poor:

a cushion with a fringe;
glass animals arranged
across the mantlepiece (a swan, a horse,
a bull); a mirror;
a teacup sent from Scotland;
several heraldic spoons;
a lamp; and in the centre
of the table, a paperweight:
hollow glass globe

filled with water, and
a house, a man, a snowstorm.

The room was as
dustless as possible
and free of spiders.
                          I
stood in the door-
way, at the fulcrum where

this trivial but
stringent inner order
held its delicate balance
with the random scattering or
clogged merging of
things: ditch by the road; dried
reeds in the wind; flat
wet bush, grey sky
sweeping away outside.

iii

The cities are only outposts.

Watch that man
walking on cement as though on snowshoes:
senses the road
a muskeg, loose mat of roots and brown
vegetable decay
or crust of ice that
easily might break and
slush or water under
suck him down

The land flows like a
sluggish current.

The mountains eddy slowly towards the sea.

iv

The people who come here also
flow: their bodies becoming
nebulous, diffused, quietly
spreading out into the air across
these interstellar sidewalks

v

This is what it must be
like in outer space
where the stars are pasted flat
against the total
black of the expanding
eye, fly-
specks of burning dust

vi

There is no centre;
the centres
travel with us unseen
like our shadows
on a day when there is no sun.

We must move back:
there are too many foregrounds.

Now, clutter of twigs
across our eyes, tatter
of birds at the eye's edge; the straggle
of dead treetrunks; patch
of lichen
and in love, tangle
of limbs and fingers, the texture
of pores and lines on the skin.

vii

An other sense tugs at us:
we have lost something,
some key to these things
which must be writings
and are locked against us
or perhaps (like a potential
mine, unknown vein
of metal in the rock)
something not lost or hidden
but just not found yet

that informs, holds together
this confusion, this largeness
and dissolving:

not above or behind
or within it, but one
with it: an

identity:
something too huge and simple
for us to see.

THE EXPLORERS

The explorers will come
in several minutes
and find this island.

(It is a stunted island,
rocky, with room
for only a few trees, a thin
layer of soil; hardly
bigger than a bed.
That is how
they've missed it
until now)

Already their boats draw near,
their flags flutter,
their oars push at the water.

They will be jubilant
and shout, at finding
that there was something
they had not found before,

although this island will afford
not much more than a foothold:
little to explore;

but they will be surprised

(we can't see them yet;
we know they must be
coming, because they always come
several minutes too late)

(they won't be able
to tell how long
we were cast away, or why,
or, from these
gnawed bones,
which was the survivor)

at the two skeletons

THE SETTLERS

A second after
the first boat touched the shore,
there was a quick skirmish
brief as a twinge
and then the land was settled

(of course there was really
no shore: the water turned
to land by having
objects in it: caught and kept
from surge, made
less than immense
by networks of
roads and grids of fences)

and as for us, who drifted
picked by the sharks
during so many bluegreen
centuries before they came:
they found us
inland, stranded
on a ridge of bedrock,
defining our own island.

From our inarticulate
skeleton (so
intermixed, one
carcass),
they postulated wolves.

They dug us down
into the solid granite
where our bones grew flesh again,
came up trees and
grass.

Still
we are the salt
seas that uphold these lands.

Now horses graze
inside this fence of ribs, and

children run, with green
smiles, (not knowing
where) across
the fields of our open hands.

MARGARET ATWOOD, whose work has been published in more than forty-five countries, is the author of more than fifty books of fiction, poetry, critical essays, and graphic novels. Her latest novel, *The Testaments*, is the long-awaited sequel to *The Handmaid's Tale*, now an award-winning TV series. Her other works of fiction include *Cat's Eye*, finalist for the 1989 Booker Prize; *Alias Grace*, which won the Giller Prize in Canada and the Premio Mondello in Italy; *The Blind Assassin*, winner of the 2000 Booker Prize; The MaddAddam Trilogy; and *Hag-Seed*. She is the recipient of numerous awards, including the Peace Prize of the German Book Trade, the Franz Kafka International Literary Prize, the PEN Center USA Lifetime Achievement Award, and the *Los Angeles Times* Innovator's Award. She lives in Toronto with the writer Graeme Gibson.

LIST

The A List